Our New Baby is in the NICU

Written by: Lindsey Coker Luckey

Illustrated by: Carla M. Valero

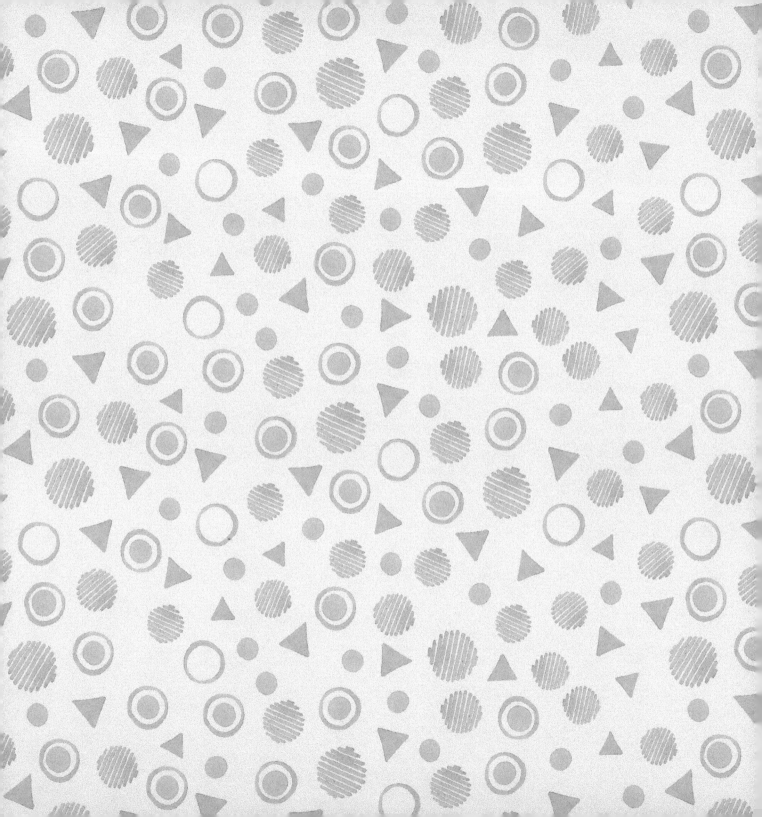

It all began on my last birthday. When Mommy and Daddy told me to make a wish and blow the candles on the cake, I wished for someone to play with, someone who would be with me all the time, a friend, a partner, a sister.

A few months later, when we were having breakfast, Mommy and Daddy told me that I was getting a new baby sister! I was the happiest. I jumped up and down and counted the days until my sister was to be born.

The days went by and then one night, Daddy woke me up and told me to get dressed quickly. I got dressed as fast as I could, and we all went to the hospital. Mommy was hurting and when the doctor came out, he said that my sister was going to be born early.

I was happy at first, but when I saw the look on my dad's face, I got scared. He explained that if my sister was born prematurely, she might not be as healthy. She didn't have enough time in Mommy's tummy to grow as much as she needed to. I could see that my dad was very worried, so I gave him a hug and curled up next to him on the waiting room chairs.

I was a bit sleepy, but so excited to see my baby sister. After a few hours, the doctor came out and told us the news.

He said, "Congratulations, you have a beautiful baby girl. We would like to keep her in the NICU for a while until she is ready to go home. Would you like to see her now?"

"Yes!" I shouted.

My dad laughed and picked me up. We went to the NICU when they were just moving her there.

The NICU is a place where premature or sick babies are kept so that they can be taken care of more carefully.

They wrapped her in warm wraps and put her in an incubator. The doctors hooked her up to a few machines that kept her warm, helped her breathe and told them if she was doing okay.

The doctor told us that when a baby is born early, they have a hard time using their lungs and breathing like a bigger baby would. He told us that my baby sister just needed a little bit of help with her breathing and keeping her warm.

We watched my baby sister sleep through the glass for hours. She was so small. I couldn't believe it.

Every now and then, a nurse came and checked on her. It was a bit scary with all the needles and tubes around her, but they were helping her breathe, stay warm, feed and many other things, so we knew she would be okay.

My mom was exhausted, so we waited until she woke up. By that time, all our family was in the hospital and they were all so excited to see my sister.

When Mommy woke up, I jumped on her bed and told her all about my sister. When she got some rest and was a bit stronger, we went to the NICU and we all saw my sister again.

After a few days, when my sister was strong enough, the nurse asked if I wanted to hold her. Of course I did! The nurse had to help, and it was scary because of all the things that were attached to her. She was so little. I can't wait until she is healthy enough to play with me.

For the next few weeks, we went back and forth to see my sister in the NICU. I waved and did funny faces through the incubator, but she slept most of the time. The doctors told us she was getting better every day and I couldn't wait for us to take her home.

When we did, we all cared for her all the time. Mom fed her, Dad changed her diapers and I played with her for hours every day. When she grows up, we'll be best friends and just like now, I will take care of her forever.

CPSIA information can be obtained
at www.ICGtesting.com
Printed in the USA
LVHW071501040222
710249LV00005B/48